FATHER
of my heart

Victoria

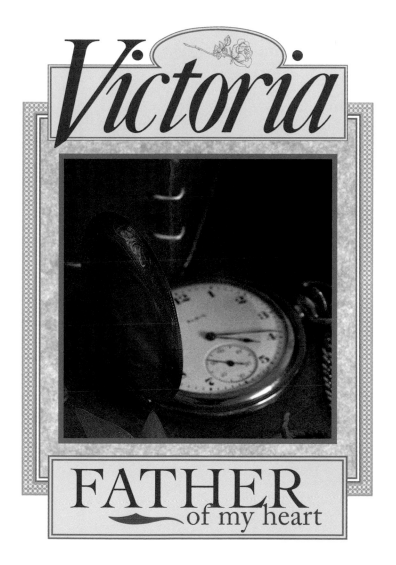

FATHER
of my heart

HEARST BOOKS
New York

ISBN: 0-688-14472-1

Printed in Singapore
First Edition
1 2 3 4 5 6 7 8 9 10

For Victoria ~
Nancy Lindemeyer, Editor-in-Chief
Bryan E. McCay, Art Director
John Mack Carter, President, Hearst Magazine Enterprises

Edited by Linda Sunshine
Book design by Nina Ovryn
Slipcase design by Ken Velásquez
Produced by Smallwood & Stewart, Inc., New York City

CONTENTS

~

Foreword. . .*page 7*

Becoming a Father. . . .*page 9*

On Fatherhood. . . .*page 25*

Fatherly Advice. . . .*page 57*

Reminiscences. . . .*page 81*

Legacies. . . .*page 111*

Permissions and Photo Credits. . .*page 138*

FOREWORD

~

Our household was run by women, as four of us out-numbered my dad. I now have the reverse situation, the only woman in a man's world. My father always remained something of a mystery to me, perhaps as I, in my womanliness, perplex my husband and my son. My father often did not let us in on what seemed to me his deepest thoughts. Men of his generation didn't, I suppose. What he did give us was his sense of values, by the way he acted and the things he believed in. And he left me as I grew older to try to understand reasons that were never directly expressed.

Sometimes it has been years later when I would see the whys. I particularly remember his way of not giving us everything we wanted in the way of praise for accomplishments. I am sure he was happy with my school success, but he always reminded me there were greater achievements ahead and that I would do far more important things someday. His message was that I was not to stop growing, not to stop stretching.

Perhaps that is why my father's closeness with me often came through his storytelling, always inspired by historical facts and great figures. He loved to read, and to share his search for truth. I studied history in college, always feeling it would be a better tale if my father were again my teacher as we sat over steaming cups of cocoa and coffee.

And so each father finds his own way to his children. That is what this book so beautifully shows. It is still a mystery to me how hearts hear each other, but they do and will. To the men in our lives, to all the fathers and father figures, this book is lovingly dedicated.

Nancy Lindemeyer
Editor-in-Chief, *Victoria* Magazine

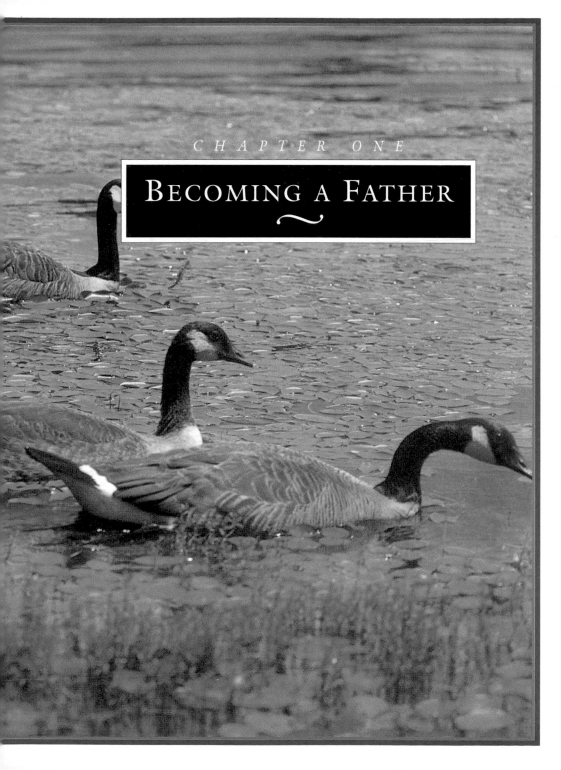

BECOMING A FATHER

~

As her term drew to a close, he cherished her more. It was another bond of the flesh between them and seemed to deepen their union and render it more complex. When he watched from afar her lumbering tread and the slow swaying of her uncorseted figure, when he looked at her at his ease as they sat facing each other and she relaxed wearily into her armchair, then his happiness could not contain itself. He would get up, kiss her, caress her face, call her "little mother," try to cajole her into dancing, and half laughing, half crying, utter all sorts of playful endearments that came to his mind. The idea of having begotten a child delighted him. Now he lacked nothing. He knew all there was to know about human existence, and he sat down before its table, as it were, with both elbows planted serenely.

~

Gustave Flaubert
MADAME BOVARY

ombey was about eight-and-forty years of age. Son about eight-and-forty minutes. Dombey was rather bald, rather red, and though a handsome well-made man, too stern and pompous in appearance to be prepossessing. Son was very bald, and very red, and though (of course) an undeniably fine infant, somewhat crushed and spotty in his general effect, as yet.

~

Charles Dickens
DOMBEY AND SON

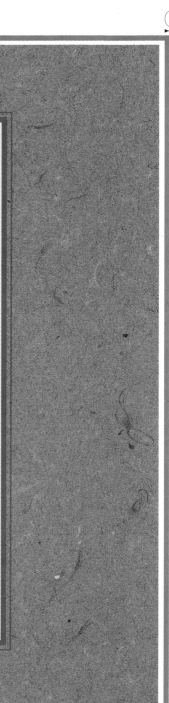

Introduced to his child in the nursing home, he recoiled with a startled "Oi!" and as the days went by the feeling that he had run up against something red-hot in no way diminished. The only thing that prevented a father's love from faltering was the fact that there was in his possession a photograph of himself at the same early age, in which he, too, looked like a homicidal fried egg.

P. G. Wodehouse
EGGS, BEANS,
AND CRUMPETS

I am just the age now that

my father was when I was born.

Jim Fergus
MY FATHER'S SON

We think of a father as an old, or at least middle-aged man. The astounding truth is that most fathers are young men, and that they make their greatest sacrifices in their youth. I never meet a young man in a public park on Sunday morning wheeling his first baby in a perambulator without feeling an ache of reverence.

~

James Douglas

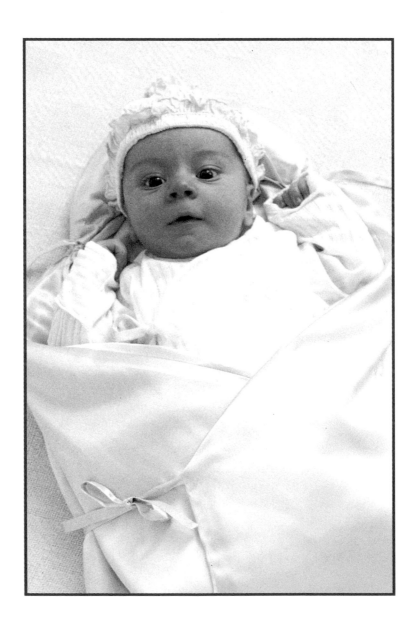

an went into his and Rita's bedroom, where they were keeping the baby for the first few nights. It lay face-down in one corner of the cradle with its knees drawn up to its stomach and its nose pressed into the sheet. How could it manage to breathe that way? But Ian heard tiny sighing sounds. Long strands of fine black hair wisped past the neckband of the flannel gown. Ian felt a surge of pity for those scrawny, hunched, defenseless little shoulders.

He knelt beside the cradle and turned the baby over, at the same time gingerly scooping it up so that he held a warm, wrinkled bundle against his chest as he rose. This didn't feel like any eight pounds. It felt like nothing, like thistledown ~ a burden so light it seemed almost buoyant; or maybe he was misled by the softness of the flannel. The baby stirred and clutched two miniature handfuls of air but went on sleeping. Ian bore his son gently across the upstairs hall.

Anne Tyler
SAINT MAYBE

**F**rom my father I learned to catnap and to tell time without a watch. My paternal grandfather spent most of my childhood trying to convince me that mustard was peanut butter and that peanut butter was mustard. It was a durable joke. He drove a push-button Chrysler and lived in town, which was as good as it got for an Iowa farmer. My maternal grandfather used to ask at breakfast if I was up for all day. He had failed as a tenant farmer and was retired by the time I knew him. His sense of humor never let him down.

Verlyn Klinkenborg
NOTES FOR A LIFE NOT MY OWN

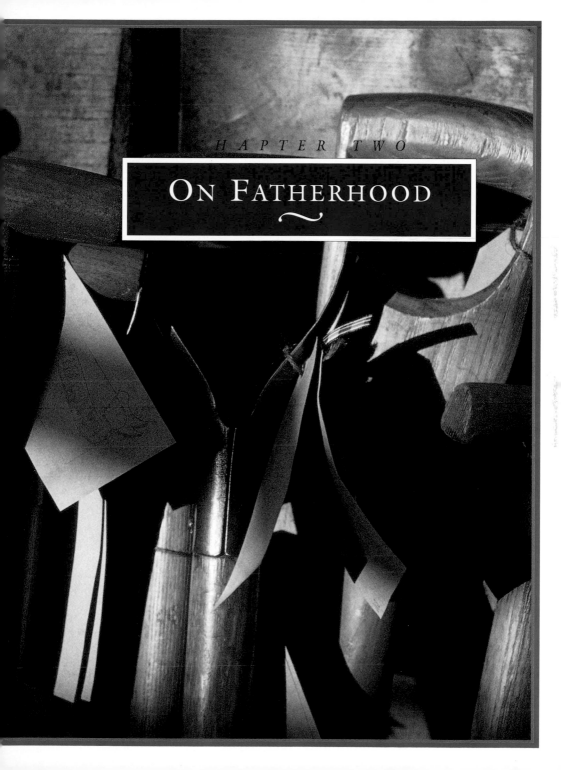

C H A P T E R   T W O

ON FATHERHOOD

Of that straight

back, strong as a young ash tree,

of that quiet, self-assured gait,

the blond hair along the tanned arms,

of the thick blond hair of that head,

hair I have cut myself now

for fourteen years, of the reassuring

voice, the gaiety of those

gray blue eyes, his mother's.

Bone of our bone. A son. The fact

the mystery we call fatherhood.

Paul Mariani
A WALK IN EARLY MARCH

See yon pale stripling! when a boy,
A mother's pride, a father's joy!

Sir Walter Scott
ROKEBY

ant had the passion of the true wanderer, of him who wanders from a fixed point. He needed the order and the dependence of a home ~ he was intensely a family man: their clustered warmth and strength about him was life. After his punctual morning tirade at Eliza, he went about the rousing of the slumbering children. Comically, he could not endure feeling, in the morning, that he was the only one awake and about.

His waking cry, delivered by formula, with huge comic gruffness from the foot of the stairs, took this form:

"Steve! Ben! Grover! Luke! You damned scoundrels: get up! In God's name, what will become of you! You'll never amount to anything as long as you live."

He would continue to roar at them from below as if they were wakefully attentive above.

"When I was your age, I had milked four cows, done all the chores, and walked eight miles through the snow by this time."

Indeed, when he described his early schooling, he furnished a landscape that was constantly three feet deep in snow, and frozen hard. He seemed never to have attended school save under polar conditions.

And fifteen minutes later, he would roar again: "You'll never amount to anything, you good-for-nothing bums! If one side of the wall caved in, you'd roll over to the other."

Presently now there would be the rapid thud of feet upstairs, and one by one they would descend, rushing naked into the sitting-room with their clothing bundled in their arms. Before his roaring fire they would dress.

By breakfast, save for sporadic laments, Gant was in something approaching good humor. They fed hugely: he stoked their plates for them with great slabs of fried steak, grits fried in egg, hot biscuits, jam, fried apples. He departed for his shop about the time the boys, their throats still convulsively swallowing hot food and coffee, rushed from the house at the warning signal of the mellow-tolling final nine-o'clock school bell.

He returned for lunch ~ dinner, as they called it ~ briefly garrulous with the morning's news; in the evening, as the family gathered in again, he returned, built his great fire, and launched his supreme invective, a ceremony which required a half hour in composition, and another three-quarters, with repetition and additions, in delivery. They dined then quite happily.

Thomas Wolfe
LOOK HOMEWARD, ANGEL

The house in which the fourteen sisters of Emilio Montez O'Brien lived radiated femininity. . . .

Even their Irish father, Nelson O'Brien, photographer and the owner of the Jewel Box Movie Theater in town, sometimes noticed the effects of their feminine influence on himself: this gentleman would move through the rooms of the house feeling a sense of elation and love that sometimes startled him; on other days, he had the air of a lost sailor looking out toward the edges of the sea. Struggling with his thoughts, he'd try to understand just what his pretty girls were thinking, and he, a brooding man, aware of life's troubles, did not know what to make of their gaiety. Sometimes, when his daughters were gathered in the parlor, he would walk by them slowly, as if passing through a corridor thick with silk curtains that had been warmed in the sun. And he would find himself sitting on the couch with one of his little daughters on his lap, playing a silly game like "smack-your-Poppy-on-the-nose," or easily spend a half hour trying to teach baby a single word like "apple," repeating it until he would pull from his jacket pocket a watch on a chain and, noticing the time, make his way out into the world to work, leaving his quivering, exuberant daughters behind. And they would call out to him or follow him to the door, and when he got into his Model T to drive into town or along the country roads to some job, they would gather on the porch, waving goodbye to their father, who at such moments would experience a pleasant befuddlement.

Oscar Hijuelos
**THE FOURTEEN SISTERS OF
EMILIO MONTEZ O'BRIEN**

hen my parents came up to visit me at school on a weekend, I would spot them way off and I would run as fast as I could and kiss them hello. Not many boys at the school kissed their fathers, I noticed, and so about my third year there, when my parents came up, I approached them slower, aware that I was being watched. I kissed my mother and then I turned to my father. He knew exactly what was going on in my mind and he waited for me to make the first move. When he saw it was not to be a hug or a kiss as it had always been before, when he saw it was to be a handshake, he smiled and put out his hand to meet mine.

Philip B. Kunhardt, Jr.

When John Andros felt old he found solace in the thought of life continuing through his child. The dark trumpets of oblivion were less loud at the patter of his child's feet or at the sound of his child's voice babbling mad non sequiturs to him over the telephone. The latter incident occurred every afternoon at three when his wife called the office from the country, and he came to look forward to it as one of the vivid minutes of his day.

F. Scott Fitzgerald
THE BABY PARTY

My father was a
true father ~ he loved me.
And because he loved me,
I loved him: first,
as a child, with the love
which is worship;
then, as a youth, with the
love that gives battle;
last, as a man, with the love
which understands.

~

E. E. Cummings

f there was a singalong around the piano, fathers didn't sing (uncles, maybe). Fathers preferred to sit in the corner talking in low voices about great golf courses they had known. A grown man who sang was nominally encouraged, but it was understood he was playing with the girls. Back now to my house, where my father is banging the piano dementedly ~ ragtime, Gilbert and Sullivan, whatever comes out of our bulging piano seat ~ as if his wrong notes were determined to be heard by the whole village. My friends, future fathers all, stand around in confusion. What kind of guy is this? Is he an Entertainer or something? It is all right to be an Entertainer. But not this stuff.

Yet after a while, they would chirp up shyly. If Mr. Sheed did it, it must be okay ~ in this house. Fathers were sacred; it was a reciprocal deal.

~

Wilfred Sheed

Daughter, dim those reverent eyes;

Daddy must apologize.

Daddy's not an engineer;

Never will be, now, I fear.

Daddy couldn't drive a train,

Not for all the sherry in Spain.

Daddy's not a fireman, too;

He couldn't do what firemen do.

Clanging bells and screaming sirens

Are no part of his environs.

In case of fire, no hero he;

Merely a humble rescuee.

Also, greatly to his grief,

Daddy's not an Indian chief.

Daddy cannot stealthy walk

Or wield a lethal tomahawk.

Hark to Daddy's secret grim:

Feathers only tickle him.

Better learn it now than later:
Daddy's not an aviator.
Daddy cannot soar and swoop,
Neither can he loop the loop.
Parachutes he never hung on to,
And what is worse, he doesn't want to.

As long as Daddy's being defiant,
Daddy, child, is not a giant.
You'll travel far if you would seek
A less remarkable physique.
That's why he feels a decade older
When you are riding on his shoulder.

Another thing that Daddy ain't,
frankly tell you, is a saint.
Daddy, my faithful catechumen,
Is widely known as all too human.
Still, if you watch him, you will find
He does his best, when so inclined.

One final skeleton while I dare:
Daddy's not a millionaire.
Alas, his most amusing verse
Is not a Fortunatus purse.
What I should buy for you, my sweeting,
Did journals end in both ends meeting!

There, child, you have the dismal truth,
Now obvious as a missing tooth.
Your doom it is to be the daughter
Of one as romantic as soapy water.
Should you like it, you'd overwhelm me,
And if you hate it, please don't tell me.

Ogden Nash
THE FACTS OF LIFE

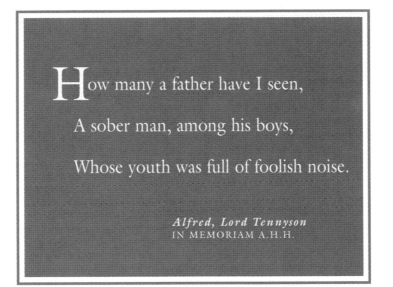

How many a father have I seen,

A sober man, among his boys,

Whose youth was full of foolish noise.

Alfred, Lord Tennyson
IN MEMORIAM A.H.H.

W e were arguing, and I took exception to what I perceived as high-handedness. "You should respect me," I said. "We're supposed to be friends."

He looked at me gravely. "We are not *friends*. I am your father."

I haven't quite figured this out, because he is far from being my best friend. Sometimes I'm not sure we even know each other. But it seems he is the truest friend I have had, and can expect to have.

~

Anthony Walton

y father's virtues, those I dreamed about, those I saw when I was awake, those I understood and misunderstood, were, as I felt them, in dreams or wakefulness, when I was a child, like a broad highway opening into a small dusty town that was myself; and down that road came bishops and slogans, Chinese processions, hasidim in a dance, the nation's honor and glory *in its young people,* baseball players, singers who sang "with their whole hearts," automobiles and automobile grilles, and grave or comic bits of instruction. This man is attached to me and makes me light up with festal affluence and oddity; he says, "I think you love me."

He was right.

Harold Brodkey
HIS SON, IN HIS ARMS, IN LIGHT, ALOFT

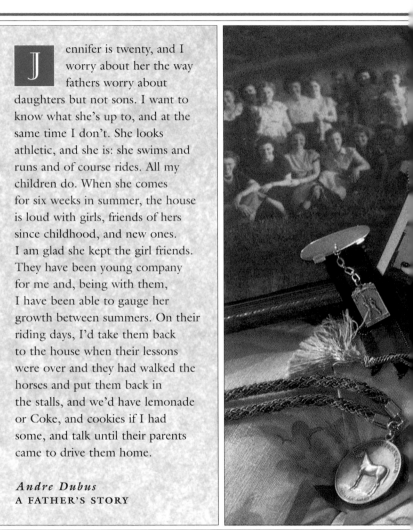

J ennifer is twenty, and I worry about her the way fathers worry about daughters but not sons. I want to know what she's up to, and at the same time I don't. She looks athletic, and she is: she swims and runs and of course rides. All my children do. When she comes for six weeks in summer, the house is loud with girls, friends of hers since childhood, and new ones. I am glad she kept the girl friends. They have been young company for me and, being with them, I have been able to gauge her growth between summers. On their riding days, I'd take them back to the house when their lessons were over and they had walked the horses and put them back in the stalls, and we'd have lemonade or Coke, and cookies if I had some, and talk until their parents came to drive them home.

Andre Dubus
A FATHER'S STORY

2 Sulyarde Terrace, Torquay,
Thursday, [April, 1866]

RESPECTED PATERNAL RELATIVE, ~

I write to make a request of the most moderate nature. Every year I have cost you an enormous ~ nay, elephantine ~ sum of money for drugs and physician's fees, and the most expensive time of the twelve months was March.

But this year the biting Oriental blasts, the howling tempests, and the general ailments of the human race have been successfully braved by yours truly.

Does this not deserve remuneration?

I appeal to your charity, I appeal to your generosity, I appeal to your justice, I appeal to your accounts, I appeal, in fine, to your purse.

My sense of generosity forbids the receipt of more ~ my sense of justice forbids the receipt of less ~ than half a crown. ~ Greeting from, Sir, your most affectionate and needy son, R. Stevenson.

LETTERS OF R. L. STEVENSON

I sigh that kiss you,

For I must own

That I shall miss you

When you have grown.

W. B. Yeats
THE ANGELS ARE STOOPING

CHAPTER THREE

FATHERLY ADVICE

~

Setting a good example for your children
takes all the fun out of middle age.

William Feather

October 24

My Dear Daughter:

    So many weeks have passed since I saw you that by now you are able to read this without your mother looking over your shoulder and helping you with the big words. I have six sets of pictures of you. Every day I take them down and change them. Those your dear mother put in glass frames I do not change. Also, I have all the sweet fruits and chocolates and red bananas. How good of you to think of just the things your father likes. Some of them I gave to a little boy and girl. I play with them because soon my daughter will be as big. They have no mother like you, of course; *they have no mother like* yours ~ *for except my mother there never was a mother like yours; so loving, so tender, so unselfish and thoughtful. If she is reading this, kiss her for me. Every day I watch the sun set, and know that you and your pretty mother are watching it, too. And all day I think of you both.*

    Be very good. Do not bump yourself. Do not eat matches. Do not play with scissors or cats. Do not forget your dad. Sleep when your mother wishes it. Love us both. Try to know how we love you. That *you will never learn. Good-night and God keep you, and bless you.*

Your Dad

                              Richard Harding-Davis,
                              to his nine-month-old daughter

There is no surer sign in the world of a little, weak mind, than inattention. Whatever is worth doing at all, is worth doing well; and nothing can be well done without attention. It is the sure answer of a fool, when you ask him about anything that was said or done where he was present, that "truly he did not mind it." And why did not the fool mind it? What had he else to do there, but to mind what was doing? A man of sense sees, hears, and retains, everything that passes where he is. I desire I may never hear you talk of not minding, nor complain, as most fools do, of a treacherous memory. Mind not only what people say, but how they say it; and if you have any sagacity, you may discover more truth by your eyes than by your ears. People can say what they will, but they cannot look just as they will; and their looks frequently discover what their words are calculated to conceal. Observe, therefore, people's looks carefully, when they speak, not only to you, but to each other. I have often guessed, by people's faces, what they were saying, though I could not hear one word they said. The most material knowledge of all, I mean the knowledge of the world, is never to be acquired without great attention; and I know many old people, who, though they have lived long in the world, are but children still as to the knowledge of it, from their levity and inattention. Certain forms, which all people comply with, and certain arts, which all people aim at, hide, in some degree, the truth, and give a general exterior resemblance to almost everybody. Attention and sagacity must see through that veil, and discover the natural character. You are of an age now to reflect, to observe and compare characters, and to arm yourself against the common arts, at least, of the world. If a man, with whom you are but barely acquainted, and to whom you have made no offers nor given any marks of friendship, makes you, on a sudden, strong professions of his, receive them with civility, but do not repay them with confidence: he certainly means to deceive you; for one man does not fall in love with another at sight. If a man uses strong protestations or oaths, to make you believe a thing, which is of itself so likely and probable that the bare saying of it would be sufficient, depend upon it he lies, and is highly interested in making you believe it; or else he would not take so much pains.

In about five weeks, I propose having the honor of laying myself at your feet: which I hope to find grown longer than they were when I left them. Adieu.

Lord Chesterfield,
to his son, March 10, 1746

My dearest Plorn,

I put a New Testament among your books . . . with the very same hopes that made me write an easy account of it for you, when you were a little child; because it is the best book that ever was or ever will be known in the world, and because it teaches you the best lessons by which any human creature who tries to be truthful and faithful to duty can possibly be guided. As your brothers have gone away, one by one, I have written to each such words as I am now writing to you, and entreated them all to guide themselves by this book, putting aside the interpretations and inventions of men. . . .

Only one thing more in this head. The more we are in earnest as to feeling it, the less we are disposed to hold forth about it. Never abandon the wholesome practice of saying your own private prayers, night and morning. I have never abandoned it myself, and I know the comfort of it.

I hope you will always be able to say in after life, that you had a kind father. You cannot show your affection for him so well, or make him so happy, as by doing your duty.

Your affectionate Father

Charles Dickens,
to his son

dee-dee.

ensible food;

suit the mood.

nter long,

forth in the March wind's

's some one

in love

The world is full of mostly invisible things,
And there is no way but putting the mind's eye,
Or its nose, in a book, to find them out,
Things like the square root of Everest
Or how many times Bryon goes into Texas,
Or whether the law of the excluded middle
Applies west of the Rockies. For these
And the like reasons, you have to go to school
And study books and listen to what you are told,
And sometimes try to remember. Though I don't know
What you will do with the mean annual rainfall
On Plato's *Republic*, or the calorie content
Of the *Diet of Worms*, such things are said to be
Good for you, and you will have to learn them
In order to become one of the grown-ups
Who sees invisible things neither steadily nor whole,
But keeps gravely the grand confusion of the world
Under his hat, which is where it belongs,
And teaches small children to do this in their turn.

Howard Nemerov,
To David, about His Education

If I should ever by chance grow rich

I'll buy Codham, Cockridden, and Childerditch,

Roses, Pyrgo, and Lapwater,

And let them all to my elder daughter.

The rent I shall ask of her will be only

Each year's first violets, white and lonely,

The first primroses and orchises ~

She must find them before I do, that is.

But if she finds a blossom on furze

Without rent they shall all for ever be hers,

Whenever I am sufficiently rich:

Codham, Cockridden, and Childerditch,

Roses, Pyrgo, and Lapwater ~

I shall give them all to my elder daughter.

Edward Thomas
IF I SHOULD EVER BY CHANCE

My son, you shouldn't have
to wait
     as long
as some to learn to love
and find for yourself
a bright, a sweet, calming wife.
There are some things not all fathers know
but if I could I would tell you how.

John Logan
POEM FOR MY SON

When I was a boy of fourteen,
my father was so
ignorant I could hardly stand
to have the old man
around. But when I got to
be twenty-one, I was
astonished at how much he had
learned in seven years.

Mark Twain

If

If you can keep your head when all about you

> Are losing theirs and blaming it on you,

If you can trust yourself when all men doubt you,

> But make allowance for their doubting too;

If you can wait and not be tired by waiting,

> Or being lied about, don't deal in lies,

Or being hated don't give way to hating,

> And yet don't look too good, nor talk too wise:

If you can dream ~ and not make dreams your master;

> If you can think ~ and not make thoughts your aim:

If you can meet with Triumph and Disaster

> And treat those two impostors just the same;

If you can bear to hear the truth you've spoken

> Twisted by knaves to make a trap for fools,

Or watch the things you gave your life to, broken,

> And stoop and build 'em up with worn-out tools:

If you can make one heap of all your winnings
     And risk it on one turn of the pitch-and-toss,
And lose, and start again at your beginnings
     And never breathe a word about your loss;
If you can force your heart and nerve and sinew
     To serve your turn long after they are gone,
And so hold on when there is nothing in you
     Except the Will which says to them: "Hold on!"

If you can talk with crowds and keep your virtue,
     Or walk with Kings ~ nor lose the common touch,
If neither foes nor loving friends can hurt you,
     If all men count with you, but none too much;
If you can fill the unforgiving minute
     With sixty seconds' worth of distance run,
Yours is the Earth and everything that's in it,
     And ~ which is more ~ you'll be a Man, my son!

Rudyard Kipling
IF~

In Africa age is equated with wisdom, since the original culture was the accumulated knowledge and skills which come only with experience and time. Old people were respected and honoured. Young people listened to them, and their advice was sought to solve quarrels and to pass judgement in all aspects of village life. Having gone through many seasons and listened to their fathers and grandfathers, they could foresee patterns in the rains and recognize early signs of drought. They knew the secrets of the animals and of the plants, the traditional herbal remedies, and the rituals to keep gods happy or to prevent their wrath. The elders were the library in which was stored all the knowledge the tribe needed to survive and to thrive.

~

Kuki Gallmann
I DREAMED OF AFRICA

One of these days in
your travels, a guy is going to
come up to you and
show you a nice, brand-new
deck of cards on which
the seal is not yet broken, and
this guy is going to offer
to bet you that he can make the
jack of spades jump out
of the deck and squirt cider in
your ear. But, son, do
not bet this man, for as sure as
you stand there, you are
going to wind up with an
earful of cider.

Damon Runyon

REMINISCENCES

hen I was younger, perhaps five or six, one of my biggest thrills was to ask my father to draw something after I went to bed. In the morning I would awake and rush into the living room to find a drawing in his chair. I don't recall any Christmas morning being as exciting as those when I knew there would be a picture waiting for me.

Russell Chatham
THE FINE, BIG COUNTRY

... what my father enjoyed
most ~ in terms of pure,
high pleasure ~ was
scaring things: I remember
one day he and
I were coming up in Aunt
Lottie's yard
when there were these
ducks ambling
along in the morning sun,
a few drakes, hens, and a string of
ducklings,
and my father took off his
strawhat and
shot it spinning out sailing in
a fast curving glide over the
ducks so they
thought they were being
swooped by a hawk,
and they just, it looked
like, hunkered down on their

rearends and slid all the
way like they were
greased right under the house
    (in those days houses
      were built up off the
        ground)
my father laughed the purest,
highest laughter
till he bent over
thinking about those
ducks sliding under
there over nothing
my father, if you could rise
up to where he was at, knew
how to get fun straight
out of things
            he was a legend
            in my lifetime . . .

A. R. Ammons
MY FATHER USED TO TELL OF AN

Home before dark. My father liked to tell a story about my younger brother Fred. When Fred was a little boy, we lived in a small house on a big estate called Beechwood, in Scarborough, New York, about twenty-five miles up the Hudson River from New York City. Once, at twilight after a long summer day, my father was standing outside the house under the big elm tree that shaded the flagstones in front of the door. Fred came back from playing with some friends, worn out and tired too, and when he saw Daddy standing there he ran across the grass and threw his little boy's body into his father's arms.

"I want to go home, Daddy," he said, "I want to go home." Of course he *was* home, just a few feet from the front door, in fact. But that didn't make any difference, as my father well understood. We all want to go home, he would say when he told this story. We all do.

Susan Cheever
HOME BEFORE DARK

O ur father had grown up a farm boy, bare feet dark with red clay, his head and heart nourished with fundamental rural truths: Idleness is sin, work is the way to salvation, loyalty is prime, family comes first.

Virtues in the fields around Winston-Salem became charming anomalies in the drawing rooms of Manhattan. Carrying entrées from the Duke family, already tobacco royalty and, fortunately for our father, also Methodists, the tall, dark and undeniably handsome young man from the South was quick to comprehend the sparks he struck with Park Avenue Yankees when he sang "Swing Low, Sweet Chariot" and "Carry Me Back to Old Virginny" at penthouse dinner parties. He became one of those people who are adopted by Society with a capital S. Eligible, well-mannered, and above all absolutely and so charmingly Southern, he began to be invited to more dinners, more receptions, more opening nights, more masquerade balls, and then to spend entire country weekends at estates with swimming pools and private tennis courts.

Which is how and why he became an excellent dancer and a tournament class tennis player: talents that were fail-safe footholds in a precarious and brittle world ~ a world light years from the back of a tobacco wagon.

John N. Cole
CONTACT

y father loved all instruments that would instruct and fascinate. His place to keep things was the drawer in the "library table" where lying on top of his folded maps was a telescope with brass extensions, to find the moon and the Big Dipper after supper in our front yard, and to keep appointments with eclipses. There was a folding Kodak that was brought out for Christmas, birthdays, and trips. In the back of the drawer you could find a magnifying glass, a kaleidoscope, and a gyroscope kept in a black buckram box, which he would set dancing for us on a string pulled tight. He had also supplied himself with an assortment of puzzles composed of metal rings and intersecting links and keys chained together, impossible for the rest of us, however patiently shown, to take apart; he had an almost childlike love of the ingenious. . . .

From our earliest Christmas times, Santa Claus brought us toys that instruct boys and girls (separately) how to build things ~ stone blocks cut to the castle-building style, Tinker Toys, and Erector sets. Daddy made for us himself elaborate kites that needed to be taken miles out of town to a pasture long enough (and my father was not afraid of horses and cows watching) for him to run with and get up on a long cord to which my mother held the spindle, and then we children were given it to hold, tugging like something alive at our hands. They were beautiful, sound, shapely box kites, smelling delicately of office glue for their entire short lives. And of course, as soon as the boys attained anywhere near the right age, there was an electric train, the engine with its pea-sized working headlight, its line of cars, tracks equipped with switches, semaphores, its station, its bridges, and its tunnel, which blocked off all other traffic in the upstairs hall. Even from downstairs, and through the cries of excited children, the elegant rush and click of the train could be heard through the ceiling, running around and around its figure eight.

All of this, but especially the train, represents my father's fondest beliefs ~ in progress, in the future. With these gifts, he was preparing his children.

~

Eudora Welty
ONE WRITER'S BEGINNINGS

ad waged a constant and, by his accounts, an heroically futile war against shoddy workmanship and pot metal. He dated the beginning of the decline of American civilization from the date the factories stopped galvanizing nails by passing current through them, permanently bonding the protective zinc, and fell instead to merely dipping the nails in molten zinc, which staves off corrosion for only several years.

Dad could stare in pain at sheet metal gutters he'd hammered onto the roof a decade ago and read the steady decline of America in the rusty streams bleeding from each decomposing nailhead.

My father built to last. He didn't build for style, God knows not for convenience or beauty, and not for comfort. He was an engineer and he built to last.

Since he bought our first home in the late 1940s, in Massachusetts, the rest of us always joked that whatever Dad built around the house could withstand a direct hit by an atomic bomb.

He seemed to spend much of his time around the house in those early years trying to divine the hidden location of studs ~ those two-by-four wall supports hidden under the plaster every sixteen inches. He would tap the wall and listen, then sink a test nail. He'd grunt with satisfaction when he found one, then drill a hole and lovingly crank lag bolts through the plaster and deep into the sturdy wood beneath, anchoring shelves and picture frames irrevocably and, it seemed, forever.

Steve LaRue
REMEMBERING

He never drew up a plan for the house before he started building, unless it was a rough pencil sketch on the back of a page torn from the Goolsby Drugstore calendar that always hung beside the kitchen stove. He was not by any stretch of the imagination an old-world craftsman. His carpentry was always from the hip-pocket, catch-as-catch-can, make-do school. He learned it from his father and older brothers on the farm and perfected it during the Depression when he had a large family of his own to shelter. Necessity determined his style. He always built with verve rather than exactitude, and he never had any feeling for finishing work. To him, a ten-penny nail looked as good on the inside as the outside. To do him justice, however, my mother says he once built her and her sister fine rocking chairs, the parts carefully fitted and finished. Nevertheless, what he liked best was seeing a building go up, taking shape. Then he was eager to move on to the next thing.

～

Virginia Stem Owens
IF YOU DO LOVE OLD MEN

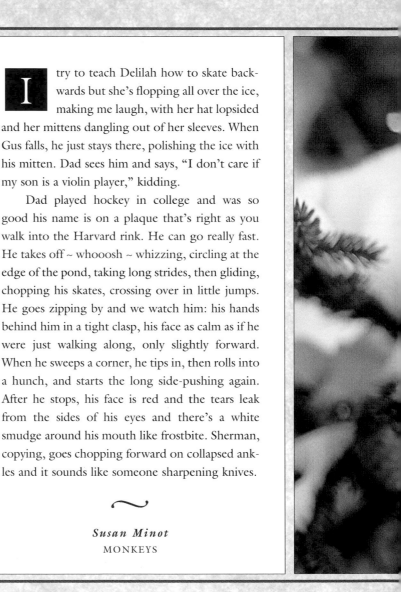

I try to teach Delilah how to skate backwards but she's flopping all over the ice, making me laugh, with her hat lopsided and her mittens dangling out of her sleeves. When Gus falls, he just stays there, polishing the ice with his mitten. Dad sees him and says, "I don't care if my son is a violin player," kidding.

Dad played hockey in college and was so good his name is on a plaque that's right as you walk into the Harvard rink. He can go really fast. He takes off ~ whooosh ~ whizzing, circling at the edge of the pond, taking long strides, then gliding, chopping his skates, crossing over in little jumps. He goes zipping by and we watch him: his hands behind him in a tight clasp, his face as calm as if he were just walking along, only slightly forward. When he sweeps a corner, he tips in, then rolls into a hunch, and starts the long side-pushing again. After he stops, his face is red and the tears leak from the sides of his eyes and there's a white smudge around his mouth like frostbite. Sherman, copying, goes chopping forward on collapsed ankles and it sounds like someone sharpening knives.

~

Susan Minot
MONKEYS

In 1955, when I was ten,
my father's reading went to his head.
My father's reading during that time, and for many
years before and after, consisted for the most
part of *Life on the Mississippi*. He was a young executive
in the old family firm, American Standard;
sometimes he traveled alone on business. Traveling,
he checked into a hotel, found a bookstore, and
chose for the night's reading, after what I fancy to
have been long deliberation, yet another
copy of *Life on the Mississippi*. He brought all these
books home. There were dozens of copies of
Life on the Mississippi on the living-room shelves.
From time to time, I read one.

Annie Dillard
AN AMERICAN CHILDHOOD

I cannot remember having ever heard a single sentence uttered by my mother in the nature of moral or religious instruction. My father made an effort or two. When he caught me imitating him by pretending to smoke a toy pipe he advised me very earnestly never to follow his example in any way; and his sincerity so impressed me that to this day I have never smoked, never shaved, and never used alcoholic stimulants. He taught me to regard him as an unsuccessful man with many undesirable habits, as a warning and not as a model. In fact, he did himself some injustice lest I should grow up like him; and I now see that this anxiety on his part was admirable and lovable; and that he was really just what he so carefully strove not to be: that is, a model father.

George Bernard Shaw

I look at the date, and it has such a look of
fullness, the fat juicy word June and then the
2 and the 4, like a couple and a couple coupled,
the whole date such a look of satiety and plenitude,
and then I remember today is your birthday,
you are 68, it is the birthday of an aging man
and yet I feel such celebration,
as if you were newborn. . . .
little by little you came back to me
until now I have you, a living father
standing in the California sun
unwrapping the crackling caul off a cigar
and placing it in the center of his mouth
where the parent is placed, at the center of the child's life.

Sharon Olds
JUNE 24 (FOR MY FATHER)

Saturdays were motherless ~ she went in to Crasden to shop ~ and my father would sometimes make pancakes and play cards with us: "Go Fish" and "War." Sometimes he would do tricks: we would pick a card and he wouldn't know what it was and then we would put it back in the deck, which he would shuffle, cut, make piles, rows, and columns with, and eventually he would find our card. All his card tricks were variations of this. Sometimes it seemed that we were the ones to find it ourselves, as when we held the deck and he'd karate-chop it, the sole remaining card in our hand being, miraculously, the one we had chosen. "Aw, how'dya do that?" James would want to know and he would grab the cards and try to figure it out as my father put on an exaggerated, enigmatic smile, shrugged his shoulders, folded his arms. "I'll never tell, will I, Lynnie?" My dad would wink at me.

I never wanted to know. It was enough to sit in the living room in my pajamas and smell pancakes and be reassured that my father was special. To discover or expose the wheels and pulleys behind the tricks, I knew, would be to blacken Saturdays and undo my father. If his talents, his magic, his legerdemain, didn't remain inimitable, unknowable, if they weren't protected and preserved, what could he possibly be, to us, for us, what could he do?

~

Lorrie Moore
WHAT IS SEIZED

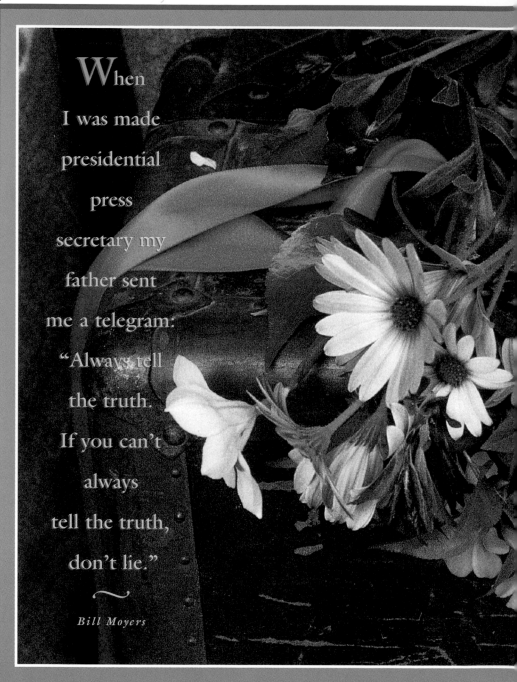

When
I was made
presidential
press
secretary my
father sent
me a telegram:
"Always tell
the truth.
If you can't
always
tell the truth,
don't lie."

Bill Moyers

Sundays too my father got up early
and put his clothes on in the blueblack cold,
then with cracked hands that ached
from labor in the weekday weather made
banked fires blaze. No one ever thanked him.

I'd wake and hear the cold splintering, breaking.
When the rooms were warm, he'd call,
and slowly I would rise and dress,
fearing the chronic angers of that house,

Speaking indifferently to him,
who had driven out the cold
and polished my good shoes as well.
What did I know, what did I know
of love's austere and lonely offices?

Robert Hayden
THOSE WINTER SUNDAYS

CHAPTER FIVE

LEGACIES

~

Who is my father in this world, in this house,
At the spirit's base?

My father's father, his father's father, his ~
Shadows like winds

Go back to a parent before thought, before speech,
At the head of the past.

They go to the cliffs of Moher rising out of the mist,
Above the real,

Rising out of present time and place, above
The wet, green grass.

This is not landscape, full of the somnambulations
Of poetry

And the sea. This is my father or, maybe,
It is as he was,

A likeness, one of the race of fathers: earth
And sea and air.

Wallace Stevens
THE IRISH CLIFFS OF MOHER

The talk turns to children and parents and families
wherever I go. On a balcony overlooking
Lake Como, one moonlit evening in the middle of an
international conference, a man from
Massachusetts tells me how it was to be a boy in Minnesota
four decades ago. He tells how his father, a teacher by
trade and musician by bent, would get up
way before dawn to build a fire and put the oatmeal on
and then go to the upright piano. One by one he would
wake his five children by playing for
each the special private melody he had composed. At night
he played the same melodies to lull them to sleep.
Now this man on this Italian balcony
during this conference has children of his own, one of whom
plays the piano more brilliantly than his father ever
dreamed of doing. Once his son played for this man the same
song the man's father had composed.
Nothing this accomplished man had ever done, he said,
meant more to him than transmitting the gift for music.

~

Jane Howard
FAMILIES

Carry on my name?
My name's my own,
struggled for
and found,
sounding only
like itself.

I give you that name

to use as a pillow
if your bed is hard

to chew
when you're hungry

to wrap around your shoulders
in the cold

to absorb the first few tears
of loss

to form a letter of your own name,
if you will.

Carry on my name?
No need. The seeds
have been
sown, and so
I'll watch you
grow your own.

Gerald M. Tuckman
TO MY DAUGHTERS ~ ON NAMES

I realize that more than any other person, my father taught me many of life's most important lessons. I was taught them with love and patience and compassion, and I know they are the basis for much of who and what I am today. So subtle were his teachings, though, that I never knew they were his until I became a parent myself and saw my father in me as I began to shape my own children's lives.

Today . . . I strive to be as careful and gentle with my son as my father was with his. I am trying very hard to be these things because I understand that what I say and do will live with him long beyond my time, just as what my father said and did survived his time. And though I know we are different, I am grateful for what I have of my father in me. It is my gift, my promise to myself and my children.

Kenneth Barrett
PROMISES

Yet in my

lineaments they trace

Some features

of my father's face.

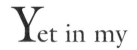

Lord Byron
PARISINA

What I shall leave thee none can tell,

But all shall say I wish thee well;

I wish thee, Vin, before all wealth,

Both bodily and ghostly health:

Nor too much wealth, nor wit, come to thee,

So much of either may undo thee.

I wish thee learning, not for show,

Enough for to instruct, and know;

Not such as gentlemen require,

To prate at table, or at fire.

I wish thee all thy mother's graces,

Thy father's fortunes, and his places.

I wish thee friends, and one at Court.

Not to build on, but support;

To keep thee, not in doing many

Oppressions, but from suffering any.

I wish thee peace in all thy ways,

Nor lazy nor contentious days;

And when thy soul and body part,

As innocent as now thou art.

Richard Corbet,
To his son, Vincent Corbet,
on his birthday, November 10, 1630,
being then three years old

My grandfather loved thunderstorms.
   He loved to see the restless weaving
of trees and all the small shrubs
        kneeling down like penitents.
   As a child, in southern Latvia,

   he used to run through the streets shouting
   while the ominous clouds moved slowly
across the dark horizon
        like a large foreign army
   coming to liberate the village.

   My grandfather used to stand calmly
   by the open window during storms.
He said that he could see lightning
        searching the empty rooftops,
   rifling the windows for his body.

   He said that rain is an ancient sign
   of the sky's sadness. And he said
that he could feel the wind trying
        to lift him into its arms,
   trying to carry him home again.

Edward Hirsch
ANCIENT SIGNS

124

I must study politics and war that my sons may have liberty to study mathematics and philosophy. My sons ought to study mathematics and philosophy, geography, natural history, naval architecture, navigation, commerce, and agriculture, in order to give their children a right to study painting, poetry, music, architecture, statuary, tapestry, and porcelain.

John Adams,
to Abigail Adams

To those who say that earthly possessions are meaningless, I offer in rebuttal that sofa. It is for me as it sits in our house a direct, immediate connection to my past. That sofa was in Thomas Howe Yardley's house a century and a half ago, then in his son Henry's, then in Henry's sisters', then in Bill's, now in my own. That sofa connects me to my past as powerfully as the blood in my veins, just as does the silver-plated teapot in the shape of an early locomotive that sits on our mantel; it was given by Alfred Gregory to his clients at a railroad in Pennsylvania in 1938 and was returned by them to his daughter three decades later, in grateful recognition of his services. Every time I see that whimsical locomotive I think not of tea, or of silver, but of Alfred Gregory, and of those who went before me.

Jonathan Yardley
OUR KIND OF PEOPLE

Life's journey
is circular, it appears.
The years
don't carry us away
from our fathers ~ they
return us to them.

~

Michel Marriott

loose in the brush pines
my grandfather farmed
learned yiddish to better wash windows
the french windows
the sixteen paned windows
the terraced windows
of a restricted town
he made violins of pine
varnished them tuned them
let music carry his daughters
out of the town
away from the farm that
burned down
scrubby pines brush pines
obliterate the ruins of the barn
the pine needles scratch the air
each time my father wipes the
tears from his cheeks
but not from the windows
there were never streaks
on the windows.

Ntozake Shange
TANGO

Between the dark and the daylight,
     When the night is beginning to lower,
Comes a pause in the day's occupations,
     That is known as the Children's Hour.

"From my study I see in the lamplight,
     Descending the broad hall stair,
Grave Alice, and laughing Allegra,
     And Edith with golden hair.

"A sudden rush from the stairway,
     A sudden raid from the hall!
By three doors left unguarded
     They enter my castle wall!

"I have you fast in my fortress,
     And will not let you depart,
But put you down into the dungeon
     In the round-tower of my heart.

"And there will I keep you forever,
     Yes, forever and a day,
Till the walls shall crumble to ruin,
And moulder in dust away!"

Henry Wadsworth Longfellow
THE CHILDREN'S HOUR

ould I ever be as good a father to Gordon as my father was to me? It was not a question I would have thought to ask myself some years earlier, although there was a time in my life (I now remembered) when I believed I had the very best father in the world ~ the strongest, the bravest, the fairest. The fear I had upon becoming a father myself was that a man could be all those things to his son and still be his enemy. But isn't that a father's highest, noblest duty to his son? To be his son's friendly foe? To create the man who will better him? To teach him and prod him and discipline him? To challenge him and make him work beyond himself? To beat him sometimes at his favorite games so that he can feel the bite of competition? To make him stand up for what he believes in ~ even when, one day, what his son believes in may break his heart? And finally, to show him how to lose, as all fathers must lose if they are successful, for what man wishes for a son who is not his superior?

Just after Gordon was born, I stood looking at him through the glass of the hospital nursery. He was red-faced and bawling. At nearly ten pounds and 22½ inches long, he was the biggest baby born all week (he would certainly be bigger than me). We would play catch together. We would fish. I would take him camping. We would build things together in the basement. I would give him the love and attention my father gave me, and no doubt he would give me in turn what I gave my father.

At that moment I noticed my father's reflection in the glass. He had come up behind me and was standing there watching his son. Almost immediately I began boasting ~ the proud father myself now ~ about Gordon's size, his obvious good looks, his brilliant future. My father smiled. He recalled that his own son had been a big baby.

Not as big as my baby.

I said it aloud, a thought I let slip before I had fully handled its absurdity. I was still competing, still comparing my accomplishments with my father's, and I had thoroughly bested him this time. My baby is bigger than your baby, but your baby was . . . me.

And we laughed together, two wise old fathers in the presence of life's new rebel.

Lawrence Wright
REUNION

Cover inset photograph by William Stites; cover background photograph by Wendi Schneider.

3: Photograph by William Stites.

4: Photograph by Theo Gruttman.

5: Photograph by Toshi Otsuki.

8-9: Photograph by Toshi Otsuki.

11: Photograph by Michael Skott.

12: Photograph by Jim Hedrich.

14-15: Photograph by Starr Ockenga. Excerpt from *Eggs, Beans, and Crumpets* by P.G. Wodehouse. Reprinted with the permission of A.P. Watt Ltd on behalf of The Trustees of the Wodehouse Estate.

16-17: Photograph by Toshi Otsuki. Excerpt from "My Father's Son" by Jim Fergus. Copyright © 1992 by Jim Fergus.

18-19: Photograph from Nina Ovryn Design. The quotation by James Douglas is reprinted with the permission of Simon & Schuster Inc. from *Fathers* edited by Alexandra Towle. Copyright © 1986 by Watermark Press.

20: Photograph by Tina Mucci.

21: Excerpt from *Saint Maybe* by Anne Tyler. Reprinted with the permission of Alfred A. Knopf, Inc. Copyright © 1991 by ATM, Inc.

22: Excerpt from *Fathers and Sons: An Anthology* edited by David Seybold. "Notes for a Life Not My Own" by Verlyn Klinkenborg. Copyright © 1992 by Verlyn Klinkenborg. Used by permission of Grove/Atlantic, Inc.

23: Photograph by Toshi Otsuki.

24-25: Photograph by Pia Tryde.

26: Photograph by Toshi Otsuki.

27: Excerpt from "A Walk in Early March" from *Crossing Cocytus* by Paul Mariani. Reprinted with the permission of the author. Copyright © 1982 by Paul Mariani.

28: Photograph by William P. Steele.

29: Photograph by Stan Wan.

30-31: Reprinted with the permission of
Scribner, a Division of Simon & Schuster
Inc. from *Look Homeward, Angel* by
Thomas Wolfe. Copyright 1929 Charles
Scribner's Sons; copyright renewed © 1957
Edward C. Aswell, Administrator,
C.T.A./and or Fred W. Wolfe.

32: Photographs by Toshi Otsuki.

33: Excerpt from *The Fourteen Sisters of
Emilio Montez O'Brien* by Oscar Hijuelos.
Reprinted with the permission of Farrar,
Straus & Giroux. Copyright © 1993.

34-35: Photograph by Toshi Otsuki. Excerpt by
Philip B. Kunhardt, Jr. from My Father's
House. Reprinted with the permission of the
author. Copyright © 1970, Random House
and Philip B. Kunhardt, Jr.

36: Excerpt from "The Baby Party." Excerpted
with permission of Scribner, a Division of
Simon & Schuster Inc., from *All the Sad
Young Men* by F. Scott Fitzgerald.
Copyright 1925 by Hearst's International
Magazine Co., Inc. Copyright renewal 1953
by Frances Scott Fitzgerald Lanahan.

37: Photograph by Toshi Otsuki.

38-39: Photograph by Toshi Otsuki. Quote
of E. E. Cummings is reprinted by permission of Liveright Publishing Corporation.
Copyright © by the Trustees for the
E. E. Cummings Trust. Quote appeared
in *Dreams in the Mirror: A Biography
of E. E. Cummings* by Richard S. Kennedy,
published by Liveright Publishing
Corporation.

40: Photograph by William P. Steele.

41: Excerpt from *Essays in Disguise* by Wilfred
Sheed. Reprinted with the permission of
Alfred A. Knopf, Inc. Copyright © 1990 by
Wilfred Sheed.

42-43: Excerpt from *The Face Is Familiar* by
Ogden Nash. Copyright 1935 by Ogden
Nash. First appeared in the *Saturday
Evening Post*. By permission Little, Brown
and Company.

44: Photographs by Toshi Otsuki.

46-47: Photograph by Toshi Otsuki. Excerpt
from Anthony Walton. Reprinted with
the permission of the author and the
January 1990 *Reader's Digest*. Copyright ©
by Anthony Walton.

99: Photograph by Wendi Schneider.
Excerpt from *An American Childhood* by
Annie Dillard. Copyright © 1987 by
Annie Dillard. Reprinted by permission
of HarperCollins Publishers, Inc.

101: Photograph by Starr Ockenga.

102: Photograph by Toshi Otsuki.

103: Excerpt from *The Gold Cell* by Sharon
Olds. Copyright ©1987 by Sharon
Olds. Reprinted by permission of
Alfred A. Knopf, Inc.

104: Photograph by Jana Taylor.

105: Excerpt from *Self-Help* by Lorrie Moore.
Reprinted with the permission of Alfred
A. Knopf, Inc. Copyright © 1985 by
M. L. Moore.

106-107: Photograph by Jana Taylor. Excerpt
by Bill Moyers.

108-109: Photograph by Toshi Otsuki.
Excerpt from "Those Winter Sundays"
from *Angle of Ascent:* New and Selected
Poems by Robert Hayden, is reprinted
with the permission of Liveright Publishing
Corporation. Copyright © 1966
by Robert Hayden.

110-111: Photograph by Steve Gross and
Sue Daley.

112-113: Photograph by Starr Ockenga.
Excerpt from *Collected Poems* by Wallace
Stevens. Copyright © 1952 by Wallace
Stevens. Reprinted by permission of
Alfred A. Knopf, Inc.

114: Reprinted with the permission of
Simon & Schuster Inc. from *Family: A
Celebration* by Jane Howard. Copyright
© 1978 by Jane Howard.

115: Photograph by Pieter Estersohn.

116: Excerpt from "To My Daughters ~ On
Names," by Gerald M. Tuckman, from
The Fathers' Book: Shared Experiences.
Reprinted with the permission of Carol
Kort and Ronnie Friedland. Copyright ©
1992 by Carol Kort and Ronnie Friedland.

117: Photograph by Starr Ockenga.

118-119: Photograph by Jana Taylor. Excerpt from *Fathers and Sons: An Anthology* edited by David Seybold. "Promises" by Kenneth Barrett. Copyright © 1992 by Kenneth Barrett. Used by permission of Grove/Atlantic, Inc.

121: Photograph from Ella Stewart.

123: Photograph by Starr Ockenga.

124: Excerpt from *Wild Gratitude* by Edward Hirsch. Copyright © 1985 by Edward Hirsch. Reprinted by permission of Alfred A. Knopf, Inc.

125: Photograph by Nana Watanabe.

127: Inset photograph from Nina Ovryn Design. Background photograph by Nana Watanabe.

128: Excerpt from *Our Kind of People: The Story of an American Family* by Jonathan Yardley. Copyright © 1989 by Jonathan Yardley. Used by permission of Grove/Atlantic, Inc.

129: Photograph by Toshi Otsuki.

130-131: Photograph by Toshi Otsuki. Excerpt by Michel Marriott.

132: Photograph by Toshi Otsuki.

133: Photograph by Pieter Estersohn. Excerpt from "Tango" from *Nappy Edges* by Ntozake Shange. Reprinted with the permission of St. Martin's Press, Inc., New York, NY. Copyright ©1978 by Ntozake Shange.

135: Photograph by Jim Hedrich.

136-137: Excerpt by Lawrence Wright. Reprinted with permission of the author.

144: Photograph by Jana Taylor.

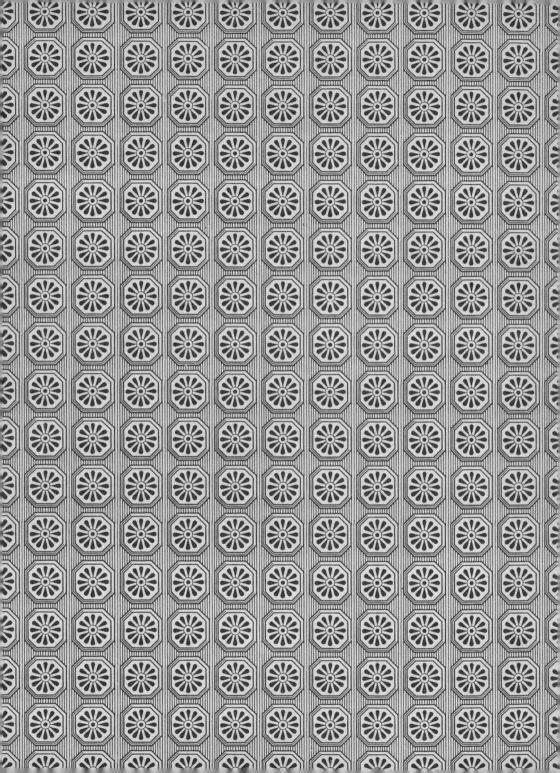